THE ALL-JEWISH CARTOON COLLECTION

(Strictly Kosher Ⓤ Prepared Under Rabbinical Supervision)

by

MORT GERBERG

With a Glossary in the back, in case you need it

A PERIGEE BOOK

Dedicated to the living memory of my grandparents, Saul and Esther Flance and Ephraim and Freda Gerberg, who first taught me the ways of Jewishness, and my parents, Lily and Robert Gerberg, who made being Jewish a natural part of my life.

Perigee Books
are published by
The Putnam Publishing Group
200 Madison Avenue
New York, NY 10016

Published simultaneously in Canada by
General Publishing Co. Limited, Toronto

A number of these cartoons, copyright by Mort Gerberg, were previously published in several of Mr. Gerberg's books and in various periodicals. Two cartoons from his syndicated panel, *Hang In There!*, are reprinted by permission, copyright 1981, by the Chicago Tribune, N.Y. News Syndicate, Inc. Cartoons which first appeared in *The New Yorker* and *Playboy* magazines are credited on the pages on which they appear here.

ISBN 0-399-51288-8
Printed in the United States of America
1 2 3 4 5 6 7 8 9 10

"Hello there. I'm the bluebird of Orthodox Judaism. What do you say you get up, you put on t'fillin and you daven this morning?"

HOW TO
BE A
JEWISH
MOTHER
Now if I can only get you to decide to become Jewish (in the biblical sense) also
Jer. 32:27

*"'Single'? With this kind of income?
Oh, have I got a dependent for you!"*

"I first felt truly Jewish when I saw Ozzie and Harriet on television."

CAUTION: I BRAKE FOR
PEOPLE WEARING YARMULKES

"It's Judith. My name is Judith. Judith Sarah Levine. But you can call me wife."

"Tell me the truth, Paul—do you love me for myself or because you think that Jewish women are where it's at today?"

"Listen, you'll take another break after Deuteronomy and I'll make you some chicken soup."

THE DINO DE LAURENTIIS PRODUCTION OF
THE BIBLE

GOOD
GOOD
EVIL
EVIL

"That was probably not Sylvester Stallone, and I do not know nor do I care to know, whether or not he's really Jewish.!"

ALL VISITORS MUST BE ORTHODOX

"But Norman, it's co-wuld! You didn't tell me it was going to be co-wuld!"

"Look, instead of experiencing me as a too-demanding Jewish Prince, why not just think of me as 'Quality Control'?"

FOR SALE
·DIETETIC
·NO SUGAR
·LOW CHOLESTEROL
·KOSHER

"Back inside, Bernie! The buffet is full of shrimp, pork and ham!"

ARCHEOLOGISTS DISCOVER EVIDENCE THAT EARLY CAVEMEN WERE JEWISH

YOU'RE RIGHT! IT **IS** A MEZUZAH!

מחזור

"So exactly when did you first experience this craving for a corned beef sandwich on white bread with mayonnaise and a glass of milk?"

SINGLE!
SINGLE!
SINGLE!
WAIT! I'LL GET MY SON!
PLEASE PAIR UP HERE

". . . and a half-pound of pain and anguish."

"Mr. Levine, may I see you a moment?"

"Morris, did you forget to shmeer Carlos for Christmas?"

"Have everything? Your glasses? Your keys? Your Jewish guilt?"

SPRAY ME
PRUNE ME
FIX ME
TRIM ME
OIL ME
PAINT ME
WEED ME
MOW ME

"Which section do you wish to sit in—Davening or Non-Davening?"

DRINK COCA COLA

THE CHILDREN ARE COMING THE CHILDREN ARE COMING THE CHILDREN ARE COMING ...

HERITAGE ACRES
POPULATION:
868 SENIOR CITIZENS
Whose Children
Never Write Or
Pick Up a Phone
Mort Gerberg

MY DAUGHTER SYLVIA, THE LAWYER, SAYS WE SHOULD RATIFY THE E.R.A.

"Of <u>*course*</u> *I'm aware of reality! I mean, we met in St. Thomas, got engaged in Austria, announced it in London and now we're getting married in the Flatbush Jewish Center!"*

"You know, for a gazelle, you're an awful <u>*klutz!*</u>*"*

"Now tell us, Davey, what kind of rock did you use?"

JEFFREY GREEN
FORMERLY
(JACOB GREENBERG)

"Actually, Artie, you play awfully well for a Jewish person."

"'Stop kvetching'? What do you mean, 'stop kvetching'! Would you actually deny me my one remaining pleasure!"

"Please wear your lining! Who are you going to listen to—me or those TV weather goyem?"

"*. . . My daughter, the model . . .*"

"My Marcia has always been so talented in so many areas. I only hope she finds a direction for herself and gets married."

"It's not a question of kosher. He's checking the rabbi's name to see if it's one whose politics he agrees with."

MANISCHEWITZ ?
ROKEACH ?
MOTHERS ?
STREITS ?
GOODMANS ?
HOROWITZ & MARGARETAN ?

"The congregation wants you to know we think you have a very nice speaking voice . . . and a good head on your shoulders . . . and you're very inspiring . . . but when you get right down to it, we don't like rabbis without beards."

"I'm not knitting anything. I'm just trying to look haimish for my Jewish boyfriend."

"I'll tell you one thing—only someone with a goyisher kop would dream up this kind of work."

"C'mon, give me 100 pesos. Why hondel so much over a tchotchke!"

BREAKFAST ALTERNATIVES

"You got maybe one that smells like cheese blintzes frying?"

A SHOCKING SPRINGTIME REALIZATION
I CAN NO LONGER NAME A SINGLE BIG LEAGUE BALLPLAYER WHO'S JEWISH.

"Nathan just realized that he's fast approaching the 47th anniversary of his <u>*bar mitzvah.*</u>*"*

"'Thou shalt give good discounts'? That's a commandment?"

HISTORIC SITE
In This House
on April 9, 1776,
Benjamin Franklin
Attended His
Very First Seder.

"I understand she's marrying him for his condominium in Fort Lauderdale."

"For my bat mitzvah, my dad is getting me incorporated."

"I'm doing the thank-you notes, Joseph. Do you remember if Balthazar brought the myrrh or the frankincense?"

"Of <u>course</u> it's me! You were expecting maybe the Messiah?"

"It could never work, Richard. I'm going to be a gefilte fish, and you're not."

NEVER MIND—
THE BRONX
WELCOMES YOU
WITH ALL
ITS HEART
NOW
LEAVING
WESTCHESTER

"Ma, what does 'kosher' mean?"

"I'm skipping 'Happy Hour,' Carl—it's Friday night—zen tennis clinic at the shul."

"I'd like fame, fortune, love and understanding, I'll have a tuna on rye with lettuce and mayonnaise, a side of potato salad and tea with milk."

"Your old Jewish mother with some pickled herring, sir. To remind you of your roots."

"I told you I don't make chicken soup! I'm a muse, not a mother!"

"My name is Morris Mandlebaum, I'm 28 years old and I want a tall, blond, blue-eyed shiksa."

"Since Lou took that assertiveness training I think he's gotten very Israeli-looking."

DEPARTMENT
OF PURE,
UNADULTERATED
CHUTZPAH

". . . so, in an effort to ease international tensions and demonstrate our sincere desire for peaceful coexistence, the Israeli government would like to invite the Syrian government to the conference table for a piece gefilte fish."

". . . and if you add wind-chill factor, the next plague will be even <u>worse</u>!"

THIS SEAT
RESERVED FOR
LITTLE OLD
JEWISH LADIES
WITH SHOPPING BAGS
AND PLASTIC RAINHATS

"Well, actually, Colin, while I don't really have much to kvell about, on the other hand neither do I have much to kvetch about."

"He loves me because he thinks I'm Jewish . . . He loves me because he thinks I'm not Jewish . . . He loves me because . . ."

"But it wouldn't really be a mixed marriage, Myron. I'm sure it's perfectly kosher for a Jew to marry a yuppy."

"We can't go on like this, Mario. If my mother ever suspected there was more between us than a purely symbiotic relationship, she'd stick her head in an oven."

"I didn't have time to go shopping, so I just wrote him a nice check."

"Says WHO?"

EMANUEL
TEMPLE E-MANUEL
A CONGREGATION OF REFORMED JUDAISM
WORSHIP WITH US
TODAY'S
YOM KIPPUR
SERVICE
WILL BE COMPLETED
IN PLENTY OF
TIME FOR YOU
TO DO SOME
HOLIDAY SHOPPING

CHILDREN
OF ISRAEL
CROSSING

Glossary

Bar Mitzvah *A religious ceremony marking a Jewish boy's attaining manhood, at age 13*
Bat Mitzvah *The same ceremony for a Jewish girl*
Cheese Blintzes *A very traditional Jewish dish*
Chutzpah *Utterly brazen, impudent; unparalleled assertiveness*
Daven *To pray*
Gefilte Fish *Another very traditional Jewish dish*
Goyem *People who are not Jewish*
Goyisher Kop *Non-Jewish head; non-Jewish sensibility*
Haimish *Homey, warm; having a sense of belonging, as family*
Hanukkah *Jewish holiday usually occurring at about the same time as Christmas*
Hondel *To drive a hard bargain; to wheel and deal*
Klutz *An extremely clumsy person*
Kvell *To express great pride about something*

Kvetch *To complain, loudly and continuously*

Messiah *In Jewish tradition, the prophet Elijah, who will come someday to proclaim the deliverance of the Jewish people from oppression to freedom*

Minyan *A quorum of ten men, needed by an assembly to begin an official prayer service*

Mezuzah *Small, narrow container housing Scripture portion, fastened to the doorpost of Jewish homes*

Shiksa *A woman who is not Jewish*

Shmeer *To give a tip, for purposes of getting special service*

Shul *A Jewish synagogue (for Orthodox and Conservative Jews)*

Tchotchke *An object of small value, as a souvenir or decoration*

T'fillin *Small leather boxes containing Scripture portions, worn on the arm and forehead by men during morning prayers*

Tsimmes *A concoction, usually food, of various ingredients*

Yarmulke *Skullcap, worn on top of the head by observant Jewish men*